Cupcakes 👑 for Princesses

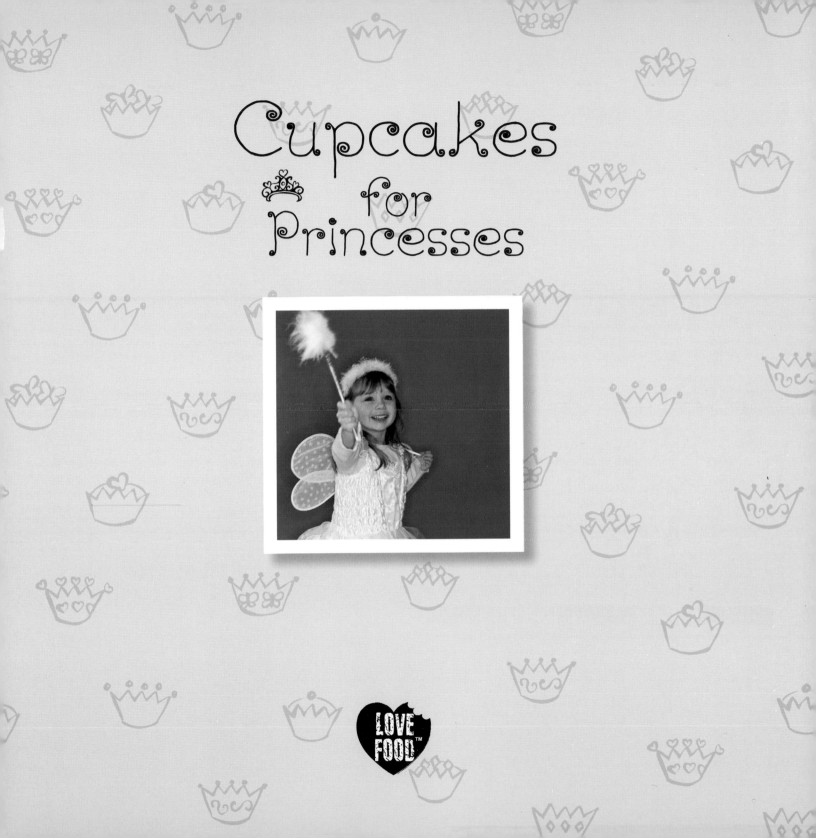

LOVE FOOD™

This edition published in 2010
LOVE FOOD is an imprint of Parragon Books Ltd

Parragon
Queen Street House
4 Queen Street
Bath BA1 1HE, UK

Copyright © Parragon Books Ltd 2009

LOVE FOOD and the accompanying heart device is a registered
trade mark of Parragon Books Ltd in Australia, the UK, USA, India
and the EU

ISBN: 978-1-4454-1631-1
Printed in China

Designed by Emily Lewis
New photography by Sian Irvine
Home economy by Jack Sargeson
New recipes by Rachel Carter
Introduction by Cathy Jones
Edited by Fiona Biggs

Notes for the Reader
This book uses both metric and imperial measurements. Follow
the same units of measurement throughout; do not mix metric
and imperial. All spoon measurements are level: teaspoons are
assumed to be 5 ml, and tablespoons are assumed to be 15 ml.
Unless otherwise stated, milk is assumed to be full fat, eggs and
individual vegetables are medium, and pepper is freshly ground
black pepper.

The times given are an approximate guide only. Preparation
times differ according to the techniques used by different people
and the cooking times may also vary from those given. Optional
ingredients, variations or serving suggestions have not been
included in the calculations.

Recipes using raw or very lightly cooked eggs should be avoided
by infants, the elderly, pregnant women, convalescents and anyone
suffering from an illness. Pregnant and breastfeeding women are
advised to avoid eating peanuts and peanut products. Sufferers
from nut allergies should be aware that some of the ready-made
ingredients used in the recipes in this book may contain nuts.
Always check the packaging before use.

The publisher would like to thank Getty Images for the permission
to reproduce images on the following pages: 1, 3, 7, 10, 24, 38 and 52.

The publisher would also like to thanks Corbis for the permission to
reproduce the front cover image.

contents

let's conjure up some cupcakes!

There's a party at the palace and we need some scrumptious cupcakes and treats fit for a princess. So put on your princess apron, wash your hands and start mixing some magic!

Baking cupcakes is such fun, and it's even more fun if you can do it with someone else. All the recipes in this book have been created for you to cook with the help of a Head Cook, an adult such as Mum, Dad or your guardian.

A recipe is like a magic spell – it begins with a list of lovely things to put in your mixture. Check the palace kitchen cupboard to make sure you have everything in the recipe before you begin. You may need to get some special ingredients from a shop that supplies special baking ingredients.

And like all good magic, you need just enough of everything for it to work. Carefully measure each ingredient in the recipe.

Following a recipe is easy for a dancing princess. It's just like the dancing teacher says, 'Each step must follow on from the last.'

Baking is like a wish – it needs exactly the right amount of time to work. Check how long the baking will take and set your kitchen timer or check the clock. Remember to put the oven on first, so that it has time to get hot. Ask Head Cook to put your cupcakes in the hot oven – Head Cook loves to feel useful!

While you're waiting for your cupcakes to cook, do some cleaning up. Head Cook will be pleased!

Be patient: opening the oven door too early will make your cupcakes sink. Remember to turn the oven off. Let your cupcakes cool on a wire rack.

Making your cakes look pretty with icing and sprinkles is the best part! And after all that fun, guess what? Now you can eat them! Yummy!

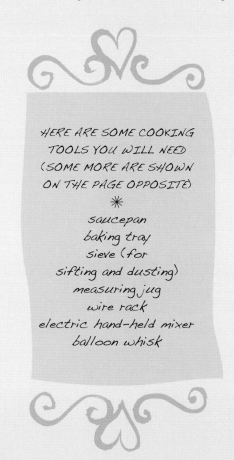

HERE ARE SOME COOKING TOOLS YOU WILL NEED (SOME MORE ARE SHOWN ON THE PAGE OPPOSITE)

saucepan
baking tray
sieve (for sifting and dusting)
measuring jug
wire rack
electric hand-held mixer
balloon whisk

mixing bowl
(to mix your magic in)

measuring cups

oven gloves
(preferably pink!)

muffin tin

wooden spoon

rolling pin

spatula
(to scoop up every
last dollopy drop)

INCLUDED AT THE BACK OF THIS BOOK ARE
TEMPLATES FOR CREATING YOUR OWN
PRINCESS PATTERNS ON CUPCAKES. THERE ARE
ALSO IDEAS FOR NAME PLATES TO ENSURE
YOUR PARTY IS FIT FOR A QUEEN!

princess kitchen etiquette

HERE ARE THE PALACE KITCHEN RULES

♛ NO DANCING IN THE KITCHEN
(there might be hot pots or pans to tip)

♛ DIRTY THINGS
ALWAYS wear your princess apron
(you don't want to ruin your pretty clothes)
DON'T touch anything until you have washed your hands (eugh!)
NEVER touch the oven (that's the Head Cook's job)
BEWARE royal pets (they love being around food—
but it's not hygienic!)

♛ SHARP THINGS
ALWAYS ask Head Cook for help
(don't point the knife towards yourself)
DON'T leave sharp knives near the table edge
(they might fall off onto your foot)
NEVER pick up a knife by its sharp blade
(blades are for cutting—handles are for handling!)
BEWARE of sharp knives hiding in soapy washing-up bowls
(you might forget they are there)

♛ HOT THINGS
ALWAYS wear your oven gloves if you're handling anything hot
(ovens and burners stay hot after they've been switched off)
DON'T allow your hair or clothes to dangle near a gas burner
(that's sooo dangerous!)
NEVER leave a metal spoon in a saucepan while it's cooking
(the handle will get very hot)
BEWARE of anything with wires and plugs
(electricity can be dangerous)

♛ QUICKLY WIPE UP ANY SPILLS
(or Head Cook will get in a frenzy!)

HERE ARE SOME OF THE SKILLS THAT HEAD COOK CAN SHOW YOU

- 👑 Greasing or lining cake tins
- 👑 Cracking eggs
- 👑 Sifting
- 👑 Squeezing juice
- 👑 Rubbing in butter and flour
- 👑 Kneading dough
- 👑 Rolling out dough using a floured rolling pin
- 👑 Cutting out shapes using biscuit cutters
- 👑 Mixing – put a tea towel under your mixing bowl to stop it moving as you mix
- 👑 Whipping cream
- 👑 Whisking egg whites

WHEN YOU SEE THE FOLLOWING SYMBOL, YOU NEED TO ASK HEAD COOK FOR HELP. THIS COULD BE BECAUSE A HOT OVEN, HOB, ELECTRICAL APPLIANCE, SHARP KNIFE OR SCISSORS ARE INVOLVED IN THE RECIPE PREPARATION.

basic cupcake and buttercream recipe
(to create your own special cupcakes!)

MAKES 12 CUPCAKES

FOR THE CUPCAKES
150 g/5½ oz butter,
   softened
140 g/5 oz caster sugar
2 eggs, lightly beaten
115 g/4 oz self-
   raising flour, sifted
½ tsp vanilla extract
1-2 tbsp milk

FOR THE BUTTERCREAM
175 g/6 oz butter,
   softened
350 g/12 oz icing sugar,
   sifted

1 Turn on the oven to 200°C/ 400°F/Gas Mark 6. Put 12 paper cupcake cases in a 12-hole muffin tin or put 12 double-layer paper cases on a baking tray. Place the butter and sugar in a mixing bowl and beat together with a wooden spoon or an electric hand-held mixer for 1-2 minutes, until the mixture is pale and creamy. Gradually add the eggs and continue beating until they are all added. Fold in the flour using a metal spoon. Stir in the vanilla extract and milk.

2 Place spoonfuls of the mixture into each paper case. Bake in the oven for 15-20 minutes, until they are lightly golden, nicely risen and, when you press the top lightly with your finger, they spring back right away. When they are cooked, remove them from the oven and leave to cool in the tin for 5 minutes, then move them to a wire rack.

3 While the cakes are cooling make the buttercream topping. Place the butter in a bowl and, using a wooden spoon, beat together with the icing sugar until you have a smooth creamy frosting.

4 When the cupcakes have cooled completely, you can either spread on the buttercream with a round-bladed knife, or make a simple piping bag (see the next step) and use it to squeeze on the buttercream.

5 To squeeze on the buttercream, you can make a piping bag using a small, clean polythene food bag (the type with the ziplock top is ideal). Fill the bag with the buttercream and snip a tiny piece from one of the bottom corners with a pair of scissors. Seal the top of the bag (remove any air first), and then squeeze a swirl onto each cake.

perfect princess cupcakes!

recipes to make delicious cupcakes, beautifully decorated, to please even the most fussy princess.

princess cupcakes

MAKES 24 CUPCAKES

FOR THE CUPCAKES
225 g/8 oz butter, softened
250 g/9 oz caster sugar
4 eggs
225 g/8 oz self-raising
  flour

FOR THE TOPPING
175 g/6 oz butter, softened
350 g/12 oz icing sugar, sifted
a variety of small sweets, chocolates
  or silver cake decoration balls,
  various coloured tubes of
  decorating icing
24 birthday cake sparklers or candles
(optional)

sparkling decorations
will create a truly
jubilant princess

1. Turn on the oven to 180°C/350°F/Gas Mark 4. Put 24 paper cupcake cases into two 12-hole muffin tins.

2. Put the butter, sugar, eggs and flour in a mixing bowl and beat together until just smooth. Spoon the batter into the paper cases.

3. Bake the cupcakes in the preheated oven for 15-20 minutes, or until golden brown and firm to the touch. Remove them from the oven and leave to cool for 5 minutes in the tins, then move them to a wire rack to cool completely.

4. To make the buttercream, put the butter in a bowl and beat until fluffy. Sift in the icing sugar and beat together until smooth and creamy.

5. When the cupcakes are cold, spread the buttercream on top of each cupcake, then decorate to your choice and, if desired, place a sparkler in the top of each.

pink & white cupcakes

MAKES 16 CUPCAKES

FOR THE CUPCAKES
115 g/4 oz self-raising flour, sifted
1 tsp baking powder
115 g/4 oz butter, softened
100 g/3½ oz caster sugar
2 eggs, lightly beaten
1 tbsp milk
few drops of red food colouring

FOR THE TOPPING
1 egg white
150 g/5½ oz caster sugar
2 tbsp hot water
large pinch of cream of tartar
2 tbsp raspberry jam
3 tbsp dry unsweetened coconut,
   lightly toasted

present your
cakes with bright
colours fit for a
princess

1. Turn on the oven to 180°C/350°F/Gas Mark 4. Put 16 paper cupcake cases in two 12-hole muffin tins or put 16 double-layer paper cases on a large baking tray.

2. Sift the flour and baking powder into a mixing bowl. Add the butter, sugar and eggs and beat together until smooth. Mix together the milk and food colouring and stir into the mixture until evenly blended. Spoon the mixture into the paper cases.

3. Bake the cupcakes in the preheated oven for 20 minutes, or until golden brown and firm to the touch. Remove them from the oven and leave to cool for 5 minutes in the tins, then move them to a wire rack to cool completely.

4. To make the topping, put the egg white, sugar, water and cream of tartar in a heatproof bowl set over a saucepan of simmering water. Beat with a wooden spoon for 5-6 minutes, until the mixture is thick and makes soft peaks when the wooden spoon is lifted out.

5. Spread a layer of raspberry jam over each cupcake, then swirl over the topping. Sprinkle with the toasted coconut.

warm strawberry cupcakes (baked in a teacup)

MAKES 6 CUPCAKES

FOR THE CUPCAKES
100 g/3½ oz butter, softened, plus
  extra for greasing
4 tbsp strawberry jam
100 g/3½ oz caster sugar
2 eggs, lightly beaten
1 tsp vanilla extract
115 g/4 oz self-raising
  flour, sifted

TO DECORATE
450 g/1 lb small, whole fresh
  strawberries
icing sugar, sifted,
  for dusting

sprinkle fairy dust
with your wand for
that extra magic
princess sparkle

1. Turn on the oven to 180°C/350°F/Gas Mark 4. Grease 6 heavy teacups with butter. Spoon 2 teaspoons of the strawberry jam into the base of each teacup.

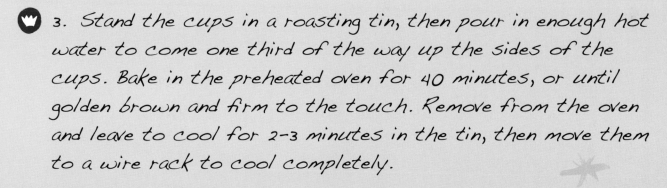

2. Put the butter and sugar in a mixing bowl and beat together until light and fluffy. Gradually add the eggs, beating well after each addition, then add the vanilla extract. Sift in the flour and, using a large metal spoon, fold it into the mixture. Spoon the batter into the teacups.

3. Stand the cups in a roasting tin, then pour in enough hot water to come one third of the way up the sides of the cups. Bake in the preheated oven for 40 minutes, or until golden brown and firm to the touch. Remove from the oven and leave to cool for 2-3 minutes in the tin, then move them to a wire rack to cool completely.

4. Place a few strawberries on each cake, then dust with icing sugar and serve warm with more strawberries.

sweetheart cupcakes

MAKES 16 CUPCAKES

FOR THE CUPCAKES
115 g/4 oz butter, softened
100 g/3½ oz caster sugar
2 eggs, lightly beaten
140 g/5 oz self-raising flour, sifted
½ tsp vanilla extract
1-2 tbsp milk

FOR THE TOPPING
250 g/9 oz rolled white fondant icing
3 tbsp runny honey, warmed
red food colouring
icing sugar, for dusting

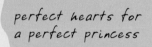

perfect hearts for
a perfect princess

1. Turn on the oven to 200°C/400°F/Gas Mark 6. Put 16 paper cupcake cases into two 12-hole muffin tins.

2. Put the butter and sugar into a mixing bowl and beat together for 1-2 minutes, until pale and creamy. Gradually add the eggs and continue beating. Fold in the flour, using a metal spoon. Stir in the vanilla extract and milk.

3. Put a spoonful of the mixture into each paper case. Bake in the preheated oven for 15-20 minutes, or until golden brown and firm to the touch. Remove from the oven and leave to cool for 5 minutes in the tins, then move them to a wire rack to cool completely.

4. To make the topping, dust the work surface with some icing sugar. Roll out just over two thirds of the fondant icing to 20 x 28 cm/8 x 11 inches. Use a 6-cm/2½-inch round cutter to stamp out 16 rounds. Using a pastry brush, lightly brush the tops of the cooled cakes with a little honey. Stick the fondant rounds on top of each one.

5. To make the hearts, add a few drops of the food colouring to the remaining icing and knead until an even red colour. Roll out the icing and cut out 16 small hearts using the heart template at the back of this book. Place the hearts onto the cakes, using a little blob of honey to make them stick.

big cupcake princess cake

MAKES ABOUT 24 CUPCAKES AND
12-18 MINI CUPCAKES

FOR THE CUPCAKES
85 g/3 oz butter, softened
200 g/7 oz caster sugar
4 eggs, lightly beaten
250 g/9 oz self-raising flour, sifted
½ tsp vanilla extract
1-2 tbsp milk

FOR THE TOPPING
icing sugar, sifted, for dusting
250 g/9 oz rolled white fondant icing
pink food colouring
decorations such as silver sugar
   balls, pink sugar crystals, pink and
   white cake decorating flowers, pink
   and white sweets, and pink and silver
   edible glitter
2-3 tbsp runny honey, warmed

TO DECORATE
toy tiara and wand
pink streamers
mini sparklers

tiered cupcakes
for a special
tiara-wearing
princess

1. Turn on the oven to 200°C/400°F/Gas Mark 6. Line two 12-cup muffin tins with standard paper cupcake cases and two 12-hole mini muffin tins with mini paper cupcake cases.

2. Put the butter and caster sugar into a mixing bowl and beat together with a wooden spoon for 1-2 minutes, until the mixture is pale and creamy. Gradually add the eggs and continue beating until all the eggs are added. Fold in the flour using a metal spoon. Stir in the vanilla extract and milk.

3. Put a spoonful of the mixture into each paper case. Bake the cupcakes in the preheated oven for 12-15 minutes, until golden brown and firm to the touch.

4. Remove from the oven and leave to cool for 5 minutes in the tins, then move them to a wire rack to cool completely.

5. Decorate the standard-sized cupcakes first by rolling out some of the fondant icing (use a little icing sugar to dust the work surface first). Use the heart template at the back of this book to cut out hearts, then use the hearts to decorate about one quarter of the standard-sized cakes.

CONTINUED ON NEXT PAGE perfect princess cupcakes!

Sprinkle the cupcakes with the edible glitter. Use the heart template to dust heart shapes onto another one quarter of the cakes, using sifted icing sugar.

6. Add some pink food colouring to the remaining fondant icing and knead it in well to get an even colour. Roll it out thinly and cut out hearts with the heart template. Stick these onto the remaining regular cupcakes, using a dab of warm honey. Decorate with the edible glitter.

7. Next make the icing. Sift some icing sugar into a bowl and combine with a couple of teaspoons of water until you have a thick paste. (Make plenty so that you have some left over to colour pink to finish decorating the mini cakes.) Use a teaspoon to spread it over about half the mini cakes, then decorate each with a pink sweet and some pink glitter.

8. Finally, decorate the remaining mini cakes by adding some pink colouring to the leftover icing. Spread it over the rest of the mini cakes and decorate each with white sweets, silver balls and edible silver glitter.

♛ 9. Put the cakes on the stand, putting the white decorated cakes on one side and the pink ones on the other. Pile the mini cakes on the top and stack on top of the other cakes. Top with the tiara, wand, streamers and sparklers.

TO MAKE THE CAKE STAND
3 round cake boards in different sizes covered in pretty pink wrapping paper, edged with ribbon
2 cake 'dummies' covered in ribbon (to hold up the cake boards)

party princess!

from cute cucumber sandwiches to magnificent milkshakes, recipes for a delicious princess party.

mini cucumber sandwich triangles

MAKES ENOUGH TO SERVE 8-10
20 thin slices wholemeal bread
butter, softened
½ cucumber

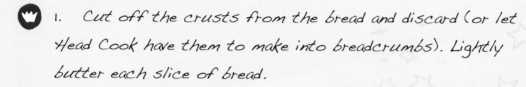

👑 1. Cut off the crusts from the bread and discard (or let Head Cook have them to make into breadcrumbs). Lightly butter each slice of bread.

👑 2. Remove the skin from the cucumber (using a potato peeler is the safest way to do this), then cut into very thin slices.

👑 3. Place some slices of cucumber onto a slice of bread, top with another slice of bread, and then cut into 4 squares. Cut each square into 2 triangles, repeat with the remaining bread, and make the rest of the sandwiches in the same way.

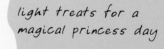

light treats for a magical princess day

mini chocolate pinwheel sandwiches

MAKES ENOUGH TO SERVE 8-10

10 thin slices bread (white or
  wholemeal)
butter, softened
chocolate spread

1. Roll each bread slice lightly with a rolling pin.

2. Spread each slice lightly with a little butter and some chocolate spread. Cut off the crusts.

3. Roll up each slice tightly into a roll, then cut into small pinwheels.

strawberry heart sandwiches

MAKES ENOUGH TO SERVE 8-10

20 thin slices white bread
butter, softened
strawberry jam

1. Spread the bread slices with a little butter and the jam. Sandwich together with another slice of bread and press down well.

2. Use the heart template at the back of this book (or a heart-shaped biscuit cutter) to cut out hearts from each sandwich.

princess shortbread wands

MAKES 12 WANDS

FOR THE SHORTBREAD
250 g/9 oz plain flour, sifted, plus
   extra for dusting
100 g/3½ oz caster sugar
115 g/4 oz cold butter
1 tbsp milk

TO DECORATE
1 egg white, lightly beaten
pink pearl sugar balls
pink edible glitter
pink sprinkles

FOR THE WANDS
12 ice-lolly sticks or
   wooden skewers

sweet wands to
bring magic to a
sweet princess

1. Turn on the oven to 160°C/325°F/Gas Mark 3. Line 2 baking trays with baking paper.

2. Put the flour and sugar into a mixing bowl and mix well with a round-bladed knife. Cut the butter into small pieces and add to the dry ingredients. Use your fingertips to rub the butter into the flour until it looks like breadcrumbs.

3. Stir in the milk. Use the knife to mix it together, then use your hands to form the dough into a ball. Knead gently, then place on a lightly floured work surface. Roll the dough to 5 mm/¼ inch thick, then use the heart template at the back of this book to cut out 12 hearts.

4. Put the hearts on the baking trays. Press a small wooden ice-lolly stick into each one (with the pointy end in the dough) and cover the wooden "handles" with foil so that they don't burn during cooking. Bake in the preheated oven for 15-20 minutes, or until golden brown and firm to the touch. Remove from the oven and move to a wire rack to cool.

5. To decorate, brush the hearts with egg white, sprinkle the decorations of your choice over them and leave to cool.

chocolate marshmallow slices

MAKES 18 SLICES

350 g/12 oz digestive biscuits
125 g/4½ oz plain chocolate, broken
  into pieces
225 g/8 oz butter
2 tbsp caster sugar
2 tbsp cocoa powder
2 tbsp honey
85 g/3 oz mini marshmallows
85 g/3 oz white chocolate chips

what can be more
delightful, for a
princess so likeable?

1. Put the biscuits in a polythene bag, seal the bag and, using a rolling pin, crush the biscuits into small pieces.

2. Put the chocolate, butter, sugar, cocoa and honey in a saucepan and gently heat until melted. Remove from the heat and leave to cool slightly.

3. Stir the crushed biscuits into the chocolate mixture until well mixed. Add the marshmallows and mix well, then finally stir in the chocolate chips.

4. Turn the mixture into a 20-cm/8-inch square cake tin and lightly smooth the top. Put in the refrigerator and chill for 2-3 hours, until set. Cut into slices before serving.

princess doughnuts

MAKES 10 DOUGHNUTS

10 ring or small jam-filled
  doughnuts

FOR THE TOPPING
2-3 tsp water
2-3 drops pink food colouring
  (or 1-2 drops red food colouring)
200 g / 7 oz icing sugar, sifted
chocolate sprinkles, pink and silver
  edible glitter, and pink sprinkles

small bites
of pleasure, a
princess will
surely treasure

1. Make the icing by gradually adding the water and food
colouring to the sugar until you create a smooth but thick
consistency.

2. Use the back of a teaspoon to spread the icing over the tops
of the doughnuts to make an even, smooth coating.

3. Sprinkle your chosen decorations over them and let the icing
set for about 30 minutes.

ice cream biscuit sandwiches

MAKES ABOUT 30 BISCUIT SANDWICHES

FOR THE BISCUITS
225 g/8 oz butter, softened
150 g/5½ oz golden caster sugar
1 egg yolk, lightly beaten
2 tbsp finely chopped stem ginger, plus
   2 tsp syrup from the jar
325 g/11½ oz plain flour, sifted
25 g/1 oz cocoa powder
½ tsp ground cinnamon
pinch of salt

FOR THE FILLING
400 g/14 oz vanilla, chocolate
   or coffee ice cream

a little bit of spice
for a true princess
is always nice

1. Put the butter and sugar into a mixing bowl and mix with a wooden spoon, then beat in the egg yolk, ginger and ginger syrup. Sift together the flour, cocoa, cinnamon and salt into the mixture and stir until thoroughly combined. Halve the dough, shape into 2 balls, wrap in clingfilm and chill in the refrigerator for 30-60 minutes.

2. Turn on the oven to 190°C/375°F/Gas Mark 5. Line 2 baking trays with baking paper.

3. Unwrap the dough and roll it out between 2 sheets of baking paper. Stamp out biscuits with a 6-cm/2½-inch fluted cutter and put them on the baking trays, spaced apart. Bake for 10-15 minutes, until golden. Remove them from the oven and leave to cool for 10 minutes on the trays, then move them to a wire rack to cool completely.

4. Remove the ice cream from the freezer 15 minutes before serving to let it soften. Put a scoop of ice cream on half of the biscuits and top with the remaining biscuits.

strawberries & cream milkshake

SERVES 2

FOR THE MILKSHAKES
175 g/6 oz frozen strawberries
125 ml/4 fl oz single cream
175 ml/6 fl oz cold milk
1 tbsp caster sugar

TO DECORATE
mint leaves

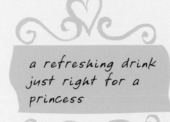

a refreshing drink just right for a princess

 1. Put the strawberries, cream, milk and sugar into a food processor or blender and process until smooth.

2. Pour into glasses and serve decorated with mint leaves.

pretty princess cupcakes!

lemon, vanilla and cherry cupcakes,
beautifully decorated with rosebuds,
butterflies and sweets.

rosebud cupcakes

MAKES 12 CUPCAKES

FOR THE CUPCAKES
115 g/4 oz butter, softened
100 g/3½ oz caster sugar
2 eggs, lightly beaten
140 g/5 oz self-raising flour, sifted
½ tsp vanilla extract
1-2 tbsp milk

FOR THE TOPPING
icing sugar, for dusting
225 g/8 oz rolled white fondant icing
3 tbsp runny honey, warmed
2-3 drops pink food colouring
tube of green writing icing

a sweet rose that will make a perfect princess gift

1. Turn on the oven to 200°C/400°F/Gas Mark 6. Put 12 paper cupcake cases into a 12-hole muffin tin. Put the butter and caster sugar into a mixing bowl and beat together for 1-2 minutes, until pale and creamy. Gradually add the eggs and continue beating. Fold in the flour using a metal spoon. Stir in the vanilla extract and milk.

2. Put a spoonful of the mixture into each paper case. Bake in the preheated oven for 15-20 minutes, or until golden brown and firm to the touch. Remove from the oven and leave to cool for 5 minutes in the tin, then move the cupcakes to a wire rack to cool completely.

3. Dust the work surface with some icing sugar. Roll out all but one eighth of the fondant icing to 20 x 28 cm/8 x 11 inches. Use a biscuit cutter to stamp out 12 rounds. Brush the cake tops with some honey and stick on the rounds.

4. For the rosebuds, knead the remaining icing with the food colouring. Roll out 12 strips of icing to 1 x 6 cm/½ x 2½ inch. Roll up from one end and stick onto the cake with a dab of honey. Draw on a stalk and leaves with the writing icing.

lemon meringue cupcakes

MAKES 4 CUPCAKES

FOR THE CUPCAKES
6 tbsp butter, softened, plus
  extra for greasing
100 g/3½ oz caster sugar
finely grated rind and juice of
  ½ lemon
1 large egg, lightly beaten
100 g/3½ oz self-raising flour, sifted
2 tbsp lemon curd

FOR THE MERINGUE
2 egg whites
100 g/3½ oz caster sugar

a tangy treat for
a princess feast

1. Turn on the oven to 190°C/375°F/Gas Mark 5. Grease four ramekins with butter.

2. Put the butter, sugar and lemon rind into a mixing bowl and beat together until light and fluffy. Gradually beat in the egg. Sift in the flour and, using a metal spoon, fold into the mixture with the lemon juice. Spoon the mixture into the ramekins.

3. Put the ramekins on a baking tray and bake in the preheated oven for 15 minutes, or until golden brown and firm to the touch.

4. While the cupcakes are baking, make the meringue. Put the egg whites in a clean grease-free bowl and, using a hand-held electric mixer, mix until stiff. Gradually whisk in the sugar to form a stiff and glossy meringue.

5. When the cupcakes are cooked, remove from the oven. Spread the lemon curd over the hot cupcakes, then swirl over the meringue. Return the cupcakes to the oven for 4-5 minutes, until the meringue is golden. Serve immediately.

mini cherry & choc sundae cupcakes

MAKES 36 MINI CUPCAKES

FOR THE CUPCAKES
115 g/4 oz butter, softened
100 g/3½ oz caster sugar
2 eggs, lightly beaten
140 g/5 oz self-raising flour, sifted
1 tsp vanilla extract

FOR THE TOPPING
175 g/6 oz butter, softened
350 g/12 oz icing sugar, sifted
50 g/1¾ oz milk chocolate, melted
18 glacé cherries, halved

sweet cherries for a sweet princess

1. Turn on the oven to 200°C/400°F/Gas Mark 6. Put 12 mini paper cupcake cases into three 12-hole mini muffin tins.

2. Put the butter and caster sugar into a mixing bowl and beat together for 1-2 minutes, until pale and creamy. Gradually add the eggs and continue beating. Fold in the flour using a metal spoon. Stir in the vanilla extract.

3. Put a teaspoonful of the mixture into each paper case. Bake in the preheated oven for 12-15 minutes, or until golden brown and firm to the touch. Remove from the oven and leave to cool for 5 minutes in the tins, then move them to a wire rack to cool completely.

4. Make the buttercream. Put the butter into a bowl and beat together with the icing sugar until you have a creamy icing. Spread the icing onto each cake, drizzle some melted chocolate on top, and top with a cherry half.

sweet-topped vanilla cupcakes

MAKES 18 CUPCAKES

FOR THE CUPCAKES
150 g/5½ oz butter, softened,
  or soft margarine
85 g/3 oz caster sugar
1½ tsp vanilla extract
2 large eggs, lightly beaten
100 g/3½ oz self-raising flour, sifted

FOR THE TOPPING
150 g/5½ oz butter, softened
350 g/12 oz icing sugar, sifted
a choice of your favourite small, soft
  sweets, such as jelly beans

a crown of sweets
fit for a princess

👑 1. Turn on the oven to 190°C/375°F/Gas Mark 5. Put 18 paper cupcake cases into two 12-hole muffin tins. Place the butter and sugar in a mixing bowl and beat together until light and fluffy, then beat in the vanilla extract. Gradually beat in the eggs, then sift in the flour and fold into the mixture. Spoon the mixture into the paper cases.

👑 2. Bake in the preheated oven for 15-20 minutes, or until golden brown and firm to the touch. Remove from the oven and leave to cool for 5 minutes in the tins, then move the cupcakes to a wire rack to cool completely.

3. Make the buttercream. Put the butter into a bowl and beat together with the icing sugar until you have a creamy icing. Spread the icing onto each cake. Arrange the sweets on top to decorate.

vanilla-topped cupcakes

MAKES 12 CUPCAKES

FOR THE CUPCAKES
100 g/3½ oz butter, softened
100 g/3½ oz caster sugar
2 eggs, lightly beaten
100 g/3½ oz self-raising flour, sifted
1 tbsp milk

FOR THE TOPPING
175 g/6 oz unsalted butter,
  softened
1 tsp vanilla extract
280 g/10 oz icing sugar, sifted
1 tbsp coloured sprinkles, to decorate

a sprinkling of
sprinkles for extra
sparkling cupcakes

1. Turn on the oven to 180°C/350°F/Gas Mark 4. Put 12 paper cupcake cases in a 12-hole muffin tin or put 12 double-layer paper cases on a baking tray.

2. Put the butter and sugar into a mixing bowl and beat together until light and fluffy. Gradually beat in the eggs. Sift over the flour and, using a metal spoon, fold into the mixture with the milk. Spoon the mixture into the paper cases.

3. Bake in the preheated oven for 20 minutes, or until golden brown and firm to the touch. Remove from the oven and leave to cool for 5 minutes in the tin, then move to a wire rack to cool completely.

4. To make the topping, put the butter and vanilla extract in a mixing bowl and beat until pale and soft. Gradually sift in the icing sugar, beating well after each addition. Spoon the topping into a piping bag made with a large snip (see page 9). Squeeze swirls of the topping on the top of each cupcake, and finish with some sprinkles.

princess butterfly cupcakes

MAKES 12 CUPCAKES

FOR THE CUPCAKES
115 g/4 oz butter, softened
100 g/3½ oz caster sugar
2 eggs, lightly beaten
140 g/5 oz self-raising flour, sifted
25 g/1 oz cocoa powder, sifted
½ tsp vanilla extract
1-2 tbsp milk

FOR THE TOPPING
175 g/6 oz butter, softened
350 g/12 oz icing sugar, sifted, plus a
    little extra for dusting
1-2 drops pink food colouring

butterflies that
will set even a
princess aflutter

1. Turn on the oven to 200°C/400°F/Gas Mark 6. Put 12 paper cupcake cases into a 12-hole muffin tin.

2. Put the butter and caster sugar into a mixing bowl and beat together for 1-2 minutes, until the mixture is pale and creamy. Gradually add the eggs and continue beating. Fold in the flour and cocoa powder using a metal spoon. Stir in the vanilla extract and milk.

3. Put spoonfuls of the mixture into each paper case. Bake in the preheated oven for 15-20 minutes, or until golden brown and firm to the touch. Remove from the oven and leave to cool for 5 minutes in the tin, then move the cupcakes to a wire rack to cool completely.

4. Meanwhile, make the buttercream. Put the butter in a bowl and beat with the icing sugar and food colouring until you have a smooth, creamy pink topping.

5. Cut a small circle from the top of each cake and cut it in half. Squeeze a swirl of the topping into the centre of each cake, then place the 2 semicircles of cake on top like butterfly wings. Dust with a little icing sugar.

fit for a princess!

magical recipes for cakes and
biscuits to make a delicious,
twinkly princess snack.

blonde brownie hearts with raspberry sauce

MAKES 8 BROWNIES

FOR THE BROWNIES
oil, for greasing
175 g/6 oz plain flour, sifted, plus
   extra for dusting
115 g/4 oz white chocolate,
   broken into pieces
100 g/3½ oz butter
2 eggs, beaten
150 g/5½ oz caster sugar
seeds from 1 vanilla pod
8 small squares
   plain chocolate
whipped cream, to serve
   (optional)

FOR THE RASPBERRY SAUCE
225 g/8 oz raspberries,
   thawed if frozen
2 tbsp orange juice
1 tbsp icing sugar

luscious chocolate
for the warmest
princess smile

1. Turn on the oven to 180°C/350°F/Gas Mark 4. Oil and lightly flour 8 separate, heart-shaped baking tins.

2. Place the chocolate and butter in a saucepan over a very low heat and heat gently, stirring, until just melted. Remove from the heat.

3. Beat together the eggs, sugar and vanilla seeds until smooth and thick. Lightly fold in the flour, then stir in the chocolate mixture and mix evenly.

4. Pour the batter into the tins, adding a square of chocolate to the centre of each, without pressing down. Bake in the preheated oven for 20-25 minutes, until just firm. Remove from the oven and leave to cool for 5 minutes. Run a knife around the edges of the hearts to loosen them from the tins and turn them out onto individual plates.

5. Purée half the raspberries with the orange juice and icing sugar, then push through a sieve to remove the seeds. Spoon the raspberry sauce around the cakes, decorate with the remaining raspberries and serve warm, with whipped cream, if using.

rocky road brownies

MAKES 16 BROWNIES

FOR THE BROWNIES
225 g/8 oz butter, melted, plus extra
   for greasing
140 g/5 oz plain flour, sifted, plus
   extra for dusting
175 g/6 oz caster sugar
3 tbsp cocoa powder, sifted
½ tsp baking powder
2 eggs, beaten
1 tsp vanilla extract
115 g/4 oz glacé cherries,
   quartered
85 g/3 oz blanched almonds, chopped
100 g/3½ oz chopped
   marshmallows, to decorate

FOR THE TOPPING
200 g/7 oz icing sugar, sifted
2 tbsp cocoa powder
3 tbsp evaporated milk
½ tsp vanilla extract

cushioned with
marshmallows,
fit for a princess

1.   Preheat the oven to 160°C/325°F/Gas Mark 3. Grease a 23-cm/9-inch square shallow cake tin and sprinkle lightly with flour.

2. Sift together the flour, sugar, cocoa and baking powder and make a well in the centre. Stir in the melted butter, eggs and vanilla extract and beat well to mix thoroughly.

3. Stir in the cherries and almonds. Pour the mixture into the prepared tin and bake in the preheated oven for 35-40 minutes, until just firm on top. Remove the brownies from the oven and leave to cool in the tin.

4. Place all the topping ingredients in a mixing bowl and beat well to mix to a smooth, just spreading consistency.

5. Spread the cooled brownies with the topping, swirling lightly, and sprinkle with marshmallows. Leave to stand until the topping sets, then cut into squares.

princess meringue kisses

MAKES ABOUT 30 MERINGUES

FOR THE MERINGUES
4 egg whites
115 g/4 oz caster sugar
1-2 drops pink food colouring
pink and silver sugar balls
  or pink sprinkles

TO SERVE
freshly whipped cream
fresh strawberries

delicious kisses for
a delightful princess

1. Turn on the oven to 150°C/ 300°F/Gas Mark 2. Line 2 baking trays with baking paper (this will stop the meringues sticking and means fewer things to wash).

2. Put the egg whites in a mixing bowl and use an electric hand-held mixer to beat them until soft peaks form.

3. Gradually add the sugar, a spoonful at a time, beating well between each one, until all the sugar has been added. Add the food colouring until the mixture is evenly pink.

4. Put small spoonfuls of the meringue onto the baking trays and sprinkle a few sugar balls or sprinkles over each one.

5. Bake in the preheated oven for 1 1/2 hours, until they are crisp and sound hollow when you tap the base of each one. Remove from the oven and leave to cool completely.

6. Serve the meringues piled up with a big bowl of whipped cream and some fresh strawberries.

sugared hearts

FOR THE BISCUITS
225 g/8 oz butter, softened
70 g/2½ oz caster sugar
1 egg yolk, lightly beaten
2 tsp vanilla extract
215 g/7½ oz plain flour, sifted
25 g/1 oz cocoa powder, sifted
pinch of salt

FOR THE TOPPING
70 g/2½ oz caster sugar
pink food colouring paste
100 g/3½ oz plain chocolate, broken
  into pieces

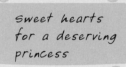

sweet hearts
for a deserving
princess

1. Put the butter and sugar in a mixing bowl and mix, then beat in the egg yolk and vanilla extract. Sift the flour, cocoa and salt into the mixture and stir until thoroughly combined. Halve the dough, shape into 2 balls and wrap in clingfilm. Chill in the refrigerator for 30-60 minutes.

2. Turn on the oven to 190°C/375°F/Gas Mark 5. Line 2 baking trays with baking paper. Unwrap the dough and roll it out between 2 sheets of baking paper. Cut out biscuits using the heart template at the back of this book. Put them on the prepared baking trays, spaced apart. Bake for 10-15 minutes, until firm. Remove from the oven and leave to cool on the trays for 10 minutes, then move them to wire racks to cool completely.

3. For the topping, put the sugar in a polythene bag, add a little food colouring paste, seal and rub together to mix. Then put the chocolate in a heatproof bowl and melt over a saucepan of simmering water (don't let the bowl touch the water). Remove from the heat and leave to cool slightly.

4. Spread the melted chocolate over the biscuits, then sprinkle with the coloured sugar. Leave to set.

iced stars

MAKES ABOUT 30 STARS

FOR THE BISCUITS
225 g/8 oz butter, softened
70 g/2½ oz caster sugar
1 egg yolk, lightly beaten
½ tsp vanilla extract
350 g/12 oz plain flour, sifted
pinch of salt

TO DECORATE
200 g/7 oz icing sugar, sifted
1-2 tbsp water
a choice of sugar-coated chocolate
  eggs, silver and gold balls, coloured
  sprinkles, dry unsweetened coconut,
  sugar sprinkles and sugar stars,
  hearts and flowers

super stars for a
sparkling princess

1.   Put the butter and sugar into a bowl and mix well, then beat in the egg yolk and vanilla extract. Sift the flour and salt into the mixture and stir until combined. Halve the dough, shape into 2 balls and wrap in clingfilm. Chill in the refrigerator for 30-60 minutes.

2.   Turn on the oven to 190°C/375°F/Gas Mark 5. Line 2 baking trays with baking paper.

3.   Unwrap the dough and roll it out between 2 sheets of baking paper to 3 mm/1/8 inch thick. Stamp out biscuits with a star-shaped cutter and put them on the baking trays spaced apart. Bake in the preheated oven for 10-15 minutes, until golden. Remove from the oven and leave to cool for 5-10 minutes on the trays, then move them to a wire rack to cool completely.

4. To decorate, sift the icing sugar into a bowl and stir in the water until thick and creamy. Spread over the cookies, arrange decorations on top, and leave to set.